Reset

Reset
A New Beginning

MELISSA MARTI

Copyright © 2022 Melissa Marti.

All rights reserved. No part of this book may be used or reproduced by any means, graphic, electronic, or mechanical, including photocopying, recording, taping or by any information storage retrieval system without the written permission of the author except in the case of brief quotations embodied in critical articles and reviews.

Archway Publishing books may be ordered through booksellers or by contacting:

Archway Publishing
1663 Liberty Drive
Bloomington, IN 47403
www.archwaypublishing.com
844-669-3957

Because of the dynamic nature of the Internet, any web addresses or links contained in this book may have changed since publication and may no longer be valid. The views expressed in this work are solely those of the author and do not necessarily reflect the views of the publisher, and the publisher hereby disclaims any responsibility for them.

Any people depicted in stock imagery provided by Getty Images are models, and such images are being used for illustrative purposes only. Certain stock imagery © Getty Images.

ISBN: 978-1-6657-1945-2 (sc)
ISBN: 978-1-6657-1943-8 (hc)
ISBN: 978-1-6657-1944-5 (e)

Library of Congress Control Number: 2022903408

Print information available on the last page.

Archway Publishing rev. date: 3/18/2022

Dedication

This book is for my children, who remind me daily that I deserve the love I seek, and to not settle until I have it. It is for my friend, Bethany, who just sees her "Mel," in any and every size I have been. It is for my coach, Casey, who taught me to just *be*. It is for Kyle, the one who truly inspired me to change. Challenging me and daring me to be the very best version of ME—no one else. And it is for Paul, one of the best men I have ever known. He is kind, consistent, strong, and steadfast—all qualities I hope also describe me.

Disclaimer

This book has stories and scenarios that span over forty years of my life. Unfortunately, there has not been only one case of mistreatment in my life. I wish that were true. There have been numerous individuals I have had to heal from, as have many other people who faced the same difficulties. The reason for this book is to help identify when a relationship has crossed the line from being difficult to being unhealthy. Unhealthy can involve one person or both people or simply the two people together. This book is not intended to accuse or call out any person in my life specifically. In fact, I even own my part in the toxicity.

I encourage you to keep an open mind and heart as you move through the chapters, because they are meant to help heal, not inflict more pain.

Contents

Preface xi
Introduction xiii

Chapter 1   The Inception 1
Chapter 2   The Gestation 13
Chapter 3   Lying to Myself 25
Chapter 4   The Decision 33
Chapter 5   The Escape 45
Chapter 6   The Freedom 55
Chapter 7   The Present 63
Chapter 8   If–Then Bullshit 73
Chapter 9   The Healing 87
Chapter 10 The Future 97

Afterword 101

Preface

All women—fat or thin, beautiful or average, successful or just starting out—have been faced with the feeling of inadequacy, of feeling less than, of wanting to change something about themselves in order gain validation. It is a vicious cycle of "if this, then that" or "when this happens, then I will be enough". We sacrifice ourselves for what society calls the greater good. What do I mean by this?

When my kids were little, a movie came out where sea creatures would trade something they had of value for something they perceived as unattainable by their own strength. They essentially traded their souls (*who* they are as people) for a dream. When you do that, you can never go back. There is always a greater price.

A close friend of mine did that. She was an amazing lady: strong, successful, beautiful, caring, loving. Yet she was unhappy with how she looked. Why? Because she had heard for so many years that she was not thin enough, not beautiful enough, and too lazy. She was told her appearance was unacceptable. She forgot how beautiful she was where it counts: in her soul, and in her spirit. If she could just make herself fit into the norm or into a smaller size, then she would have value.

She had gastric bypass surgery, which, in all honesty, I have thought of at times. She lost weight. She gained confidence. But what she also lost was her life. It took time. At first, she began to bruise easily, then she began to grow tired quickly. It ended with liver failure and death—all because she felt in her heart that the only way to be happy, to truly live life, was to look a certain way. Hers was a life cut short. Eight years was all she had. It was a tragedy.

I, along with many women, struggle with value. I struggle with feeling worthy and desirable. I know I am not the only one—there are many women out there who do. Even if they *do* look beautiful, they struggle with something else: acne, bad hair, or whatever external flaws they perceive.

We *have* to get to the point where we *know* we are valuable just because we *are*. We have to get to the place where we shut off the outside voices and the negativity, and begin to truly listen to our inner selves. We must listen to our inner selves saying, "You've got this," "You are one of a kind," and "You *do* have value."

I am so passionate about this, ladies. I know we have all felt overlooked, abandoned, or rejected at some point in our lives. It doesn't have to be this way. If you do nothing else this week, look at yourself in the mirror—really look. Appreciate all you have been through. See yourself through *your* eyes, not the eyes of society, your parents, your kids, or even your loved one. Be proud of who *you* were created to be. There is only *one* like you in all of time—ever. Think about that! Soak it in. Don't resist it. Don't minimize it with any "yeah, but…"s. Just breathe in the positive and let go of the negative.

Introduction

I began this journey over two years ago. I had written a book about not letting circumstances define you. I was feeling fairly accomplished. I had good book sales. I was being asked to speak at different conferences and give a few radio interviews in order to share my story and hopefully inspire readers. I was confident that I would reach hundreds of thousands of people with my story, so it was time to embark on a new adventure.

My new mission was to prove to everyone my worth, as if just being myself was not enough. I was determined to become valuable regardless of how I looked on the outside. I had been unhappy with my weight for most of my life and believed everyone I met judged me based solely on my appearance. To say I had a chip on my shoulder would be an understatement. I was going to call the book *You Are More: Made Original Regardless of Expectations*. I truly believed this would make a huge impact on others' lives.

I was excited and on fire. I packed up my life in one state and headed south to start fresh. I left most everything behind, including those who truly did love me. I packed whatever would fit in my car and I was on my way. I was on a new quest, a new journey—one I was ready to share with everyone.

I had much to accomplish: setting up a base for my speaking engagements, finishing up the manuscripts for publishing, and beginning to truly enjoy life. Much to my dismay and disappointment,

I soon found myself ensnared in another unhealthy relationship. I realized that I was repeating the same pattern as before, just with a new face in a new place. I was devastated. I was angry. I tried desperately to find my way out, only to become stuck.

People say your biggest test comes after success. Mine definitely did. I failed my test. But I am here to say we all make mistakes, even when we know better. Do not give up, even when you fail. My close friend Paul always says, "Just because you make a mistake, it does not mean you failed. As long as you learn, it is just a lesson in what *not* to do next time."

This book is a revision of *You Are More*. It is a story of how, even with the best of intentions, you can fall flat on your face—again. It is about how you can find yourself repeating cycles that you thought you had overcome, whether in relationships, dieting, job choices, or other areas. It is the old and the new thinking I have had combined. It talks about what images of yourself you have to overcome to become healthy, how we can body shame ourselves, and how we can allow someone else's opinions define us.

It is not just a "whiny autobiography," as my last book was described. It will give you helpful hints and revelations that I have discovered in this process. And my biggest hope is that it does, in fact, make a difference in the lives of those who read it.

1
The Inception

Looking through old photos, I see that for the majority of my life I have struggled with being overweight. As a child, I was tiny. I was both a gymnast and a softball player. My favorite things to do for fun were swimming and roller skating. I could even do the splits under the limbo bar! I spent most of my summer hours away from the house, only returning when it got dark. There were many reasons I found so much pleasure in being away.

I grew up in a home where food was comfort. The environment was chaotic and at times abusive. It is crazy to say, but my fondest and warmest memories as a young girl were of going to McDonald's on a rainy day. In fact, I loved it so much that I bought a Barbie version of McDonald's to play with.

The trips to McDonald's were a special treat. I loved seeing what surprise was inside my Happy Meal. The very name connoted joy for me. How could I *not* want a Happy Meal, especially when so much in my life was not happy? I would tear into that cardboard box with excitement and anticipation. I always got a cheeseburger with no onions. I remember ripping open the yellow wrapper, taking the first bite, feeling the warmth of the burger sliding down my throat, tasting the saltiness on my lips from the soft, hot french fries, and savoring that perfect, fizzy soda with just enough sweetness.

Just thinking about it brings me back to riding in the Corvette with my mom. She would actually let me ride in the front when we went to get these rainy-day treats. I was usually made to lie down in the back, as my older brother always rode shotgun. But not today. Today, I was able to watch the raindrops hit the windshield and feel like I mattered. There was comfort in McDonald's, in the hot, fresh food, in the melancholy day, in being in the front seat with my mom, and in the combination of it all. Since then, I have always associated McDonald's with that moment of acceptance, that moment of feeling valued. It was an emotional bond I formed unconsciously. So whenever I felt a little less than or discouraged, I would find myself running to get those fries, or Shamrock Shake. It would ease my aching soul.

I know now that we make these bonds or subconscious connections to help us in times of discomfort. We develop a relationship with food—and my relationship with food became very unhealthy.

As time moved on, the chaos of my life grew and I would often find myself looking for comfort. If I could not find it anywhere else, I always knew food would be there for me. It wouldn't judge or criticize or hurt me. It would simply exist. And I would consume as much as I needed to feel full. But that fullness soon faded into absolute nothingness. It was a vicious cycle of binging and purging, of rewarding and punishing myself with food. I was left to wonder if, and how, I could finally heal the brokenness I held inside.

It became a true issue when I turned thirteen, and the mother of one of my friends warned us that we would be "little heifers" if we continued to eat macaroni and cheese all the time. Until that day, I had never even considered that what type of food I ate would affect me. I quickly learned that food, while it was my comfort, was *not* my friend. It became my enemy. I would not allow it into my life because I knew it would end up hurting me and negatively affect how others saw me. I had to decide between feeling safe on the inside and looking good on the outside. As a people-pleaser, I decided on the latter. I became anorexic and bulimic. I stood on my scale at least ten times a day. Gaining one pound would send me spiraling into searching for laxatives or using my own finger down my throat in order to get back to where I felt I needed to be.

It became a game of control—one where I was the mastermind. If I was out with friends, I indulged. But then I quietly excused myself to "use the restroom," and the deed was done. Or I would simply tell them I had already had a full meal prior to our meeting, and none would be the wiser—well, until I lost over twenty-five pounds in less than two weeks. Eyebrows were raised along with questions from concerned loved ones. I quickly learned that I had to be more covert. I had to maintain it, and make no drastic changes. I felt powerful. I felt that I had finally gotten my life together. I wore the right-sized clothing. I loved the looks of affirmation I received from men in my life. Yet when I gazed at my reflection in the mirror, I still hated what I saw.

My eyes grew dim. They had once danced in the light, and now they simply were void and glazed. My legs were still stocky, even if not too big. They did not have that long, lean look I coveted. My butt—well, it was still just as curvy and round (this was *not* the era when robust rears were desirable). And no matter what I did, my chest was never ever the perfect size. I had spent years up and down, binging and purging, experiencing success and failure, and I was tired. I never measured up. I knew it in my heart and felt it in my soul.

I was lost. I was in a sea of confusion and sadness. I was surrounded by others, yet I'd never felt so alone.

I moved in this fog for decades, from junior high to high school and then college. I went into motherhood hating myself. I felt guilty for loving food. I felt that it was my only true pleasure but one that I couldn't have because it would cause me pain in the end.

During every pregnancy I would stand on the scale, measuring the weight. I was horrified with every pound. I heard the voices in my head say, "Every pound you gain, you will have to work twice as hard to lose." I gained thirty-five pounds with my daughter and had to wear my husband's jeans postpartum. It was awful. I was so embarrassed. And then I had to hear how a lady I knew *lost* eleven pounds when she gave birth. Ugh. I became obsessed, so obsessed I actually threw the scale away! When my daughter was only six months old, I faced the first betrayal.

I betrayed myself. I allowed myself to believe that my body and my exterior had changed the dynamic of my marriage. I became even more insecure, looking for any sign of change regarding who I was. You can actually set yourself up for disaster when you focus too much on something and when you become obsessed with it as I had done.

I just knew it was because I wasn't good enough any longer. I had grown soft. My stomach had stretch marks that looked like a McNally road map. My close friend tried consoling me. We made a pact to get skinny together. And we did. That was the only thing I could think about. I counted carbs, I measured, and I even counted points. It all worked, so I thought I was in the clear.

But the irony of it all is that neither of our marriages survived. It didn't matter that we lost weight. It didn't matter that we gave our all. Why? Because if a relationship is solely founded on the external, it can never survive. There are four parts to all of us: body, soul, mind, and spirit. I was so focused on my body that I lost my soul. My mind was compulsive, always thinking about the negative. And my spirit was broken into a million pieces. I could not be a whole healthy person because my self-care was only in part.

What good is it to gain external acceptance only to lose *who* you are?

I have two beautiful daughters, five amazing sons (three by birth and two by marriage), and one grandson who is ten. I *never* want them to question their worth based on their exterior.

It isn't just girls who face body-shaming or self-worth issues. I know a boy who is at that stage in boyhood where he is a little bulky but will quickly shoot up in height. He came home from school and told a story of how kids would tease him about his weight. His response to me was so precious. He said, quite simply, "I don't care really. Because I know what it's like to be hungry and not have food." (He had just changed homes. He'd previously lived with his biological mother, who struggled financially as a single mom.) So you never know the where or the why of someone else's life. What may make you feel good won't make another feel good. What bothers you may be exactly what another needs to survive.

I sometimes think that I have held on to being overweight because it is safer for me. I know that to most men it is a turn-off. Therefore, I can rest easy knowing if someone comes into my life and accepts me as I am, then he truly loves *me*, not who I can be to them. I know this sounds ridiculous. But seriously, if anyone knows me, they know that I can accomplish anything I set my mind to. I do not give up, but this struggle has been lifelong. So I question whether I use my weight to protect myself. Just food for thought.

We are all born with value. We all start out with a strong sense of self, of knowing what we need and want out of life. (Look at any toddler throwing a fit about that candy you won't get for him or her.) But somewhere in time, some of us lose knowledge of the fact that we deserve to be happy and taken care of, and we begin to believe others are more important and have more value. We look at what someone else has—better looks, better car, bigger house, better job, and the list goes on—when *not* one of those things can define our worth.

We fight for things to help us fill that void. We don't look within. We don't look at ourselves and believe the best is in us. No, instead we seek the approval of others—external validation. And we will never be full of the acceptance of another person. We will only find self-worth when we accept who we are, when we know in *our* hearts we are a good people and deserve to be treated with respect regardless of what others think or say.

Let's be brutally honest for a moment. Most people are *not* very accepting. A lot of society today is conditional. Love becomes transactional: if you do this, then I will do that. Love was never meant to be that. It is not supposed to have conditions. It is rare to find people who will love and accept you for who you are, who will not judge your looks, your life, or your mistakes. So when you do, hold on to them for dear life because they are *rare*. They are gifts.

I wish for just a moment in time people could see the inside on the outside, and then I believe the truth would be apparent.

Those who appear to have it together—a perfect body, beautiful face, great house, job, or whatever—how empty are they on the inside? I have heard that the ones who post the most on social media about being happy are generally the least happy. It is like we believe that if we say it enough to ourselves, we may actually believe it.

Many of those who try so desperately to be the best version of themselves, constantly giving and loving, only want to see another person happy. They are the ones with the true treasure. They have deep love and commitment in their hearts. Unfortunately, the ones who struggle with feeling good about themselves tend to give the most of themselves because they don't truly believe they are worthy of receiving love. They believe the lie—and it is a lie.

Self-worth can only come from inside. I have learned that in order to be the healthiest version of myself, I have to set boundaries. I have to say no. I have to put myself first.

Only you get to decide how you can be treated. Only you get to choose, and it isn't easy. It hurts to let go of people. It sucks that you seem to be overlooked and not appreciated. It is painful. But knowing you deserve the best—*yes you do*—will make setting the boundaries easier. Everyone deserves to be loved and cared for and seen for who they truly are, not who they are on the outside or who they are on social media view, but who they are at the core. We all have a soul, and it is precious.

It is one of a kind. It is rare.

1. *Where did your belief in yourself originate?*
   Can you remember a specific time or event? Try to go back to that. Remember how you felt. Write it down. Then write down what you can do to counteract that feeling of having no self-worth. Focus on the alternative of what could have been, and forgive whoever is in the story, even if it is you.

2. *What do you do to advocate for yourself?*
   Make a list of absolutes in your life—deal breakers. No matter what, do not ever violate that list. (You can adjust it and make changes as you grow and evolve.)

3. *What do you use to cope with disappointment that is unhealthy?*
   Find an alternative. Mine is going to the beach and getting my feet in the water. It can be anything: reading a book, calling a friend, or watering your plants. I recently bought myself an aloe vera plant and named it Vera so that we could grow together. Yes, I chose a healing plant on purpose. I have found that when you are intentional in your actions and decisions, they tend to work more effectively.

2
The Gestation

I love Pinterest and I love motivational quotations. I have them written on sticky notes, in my work notebook, and even on my bathroom mirror sometimes. I post them on social media and drive my kids nuts with them. I do this because they are reminders to me. They tell me things I think I already know but would not necessarily live out. These words of encouragement are head knowledge, but my heart still struggles with them. I force myself to look at them constantly, knowing that eventually it will all sink in. I will absorb it and it won't be just knowledge, but I will experience the reality of the words.

    I need to constantly look at the positive. Even if I don't feel it yet, I have those words before my eyes in order to make myself hopeful that things will get better. I am still a work in progress, and I have not finished my journey even though I have come a long way in the process. I had years of negativity and decades of no self-worth, and I know these do not just disappear because I want them to. I have to intentionally seek to change the way I think, the way I see myself, and what I allow to define me.

Many things can define us if we allow them to. They include our figures, our life circumstances, our financial success or lack thereof, our social status, or other people's opinions. The list can go on and on. But we have to come to a place where we get to define who we are. We are the authors of our own fates, of our own stories. We have to be the ones to set the tone for our lives. We set boundaries and live inside of them. It is safe and it is healthy, and it is only in this that we can truly find happiness and fulfillment and peace

Growing up, I allowed circumstances and others to define me. I saw myself as unwanted and unworthy. When I looked in the mirror, all I saw was ugliness. I saw rejection, loss, fear, abandonment, and torment. I could excel at school or work and achieve every goal set before me, yet I still saw the negative. I saw the failures and the shortcomings and the missed opportunities. I was trapped in my past hurts from my childhood. And I was literally running in circles trying to run from my past but recreating the same hurts by my current choices.

I had someone recently ask if I was "emotionally available," and it made me sit back and think long and hard about how to answer.

Would I like to say yes? Absolutely! But before I did that I looked up its definition. To be "unavailable emotionally" means you are one who creates a barrier with others in an effort to avoid emotional intimacy. Emotional intimacy is where we as people let down our guards. We have transparency and openness which draws us closer to those in our lives. It involves being real. It requires trust and belief in someone else to have our best interest at heart. It involves risk.

I do not believe I have been completely emotionally available for my entire life. I can remember in almost every relationship, even friendships, where I have just been waiting for the other shoe to drop. I expected people in my life to leave or to hurt me. I only let them in so far. I only exposed so much of my heart. When you do this, you create a barrier. You not only keep people out, but you end up isolating yourself, creating incredible loneliness.

I think in today's society it is very easy to disconnect from others. We use social media to tell our lives, if you will. We share our humor, political beliefs, family pictures, social status, and even sometimes our disappointments. But we aren't truly connecting with others at all. We are simply looking and liking what acquaintances post. We may comment here and there but it is a cheap and easy way of feeling like others know us.

There is always a barrier to keep you and them at a safe distance.

I believe others' hearts cry for what I also want—to be seen and heard and known and most of all accepted for who they are. The real them. The times when they are most vulnerable because there is no pretense or protection. We all have insecurities and failures. We all have struggles, but more importantly, we all have something to share and something to give to others. And my desire is to be seen for who I am, good and bad, put together and a total mess.

I am blessed because I have a handful of really great people in my life now. They have been there in my most devastating moments and encouraged me. They have also cheered me on and celebrated my successes. I have learned to humble myself and ask for help, to allow them to see my insecurities. And they have proven they are trustworthy to handle my heart with care.

So, in answer to the question whether I am emotionally available, the answer is to the *right* people, yes I am absolutely available. But I have finally learned to not allow everyone to have access to my heart because they have not earned it. And I have to protect it until I see that they can be trusted to care for it and protect it as well.

It has been a process, because I truly love to love. I want to be the best person I can be to all who I encounter. But I had to learn to be that for myself as well. I had to love myself—each and every part—even the things I wish I could change.

"I love who I am." Can you say that to yourself? Truly?

I was going through my writings a few days ago and came across something I had forgotten I wrote. It was so full of truth, of what I have been journeying through, that I just started laughing hysterically. I literally could not stop. I connected with the words on the page and felt such amazing pride in my revelation. I said out loud, "I love myself!" and I truly meant it. This was a first for me. I had genuine appreciation for the gift that I am, and saw myself as I am, not as who I felt the world could not accept. I knew I had grown. Emotionally, I was healing. It was an awesome feeling.

Being emotionally healthy—what does that even look like? I took a class about five years ago to become emotionally healthy. The instructor walked us through certain circumstances and told us the correct responses. It was clear what I was doing wasn't working, but what the course failed to do is help me understand *why* I was responding the way I was. So my biggest struggle was how I could change when I didn't even know what was causing me to be this way.

I had to know. I had to understand what was so broken in me that I would respond so negatively to people I loved so dearly. I did what I always do in these times—I researched. I read. I forced myself to look within. Because what is within will always find a way to manifest itself, and I want to be healthy.

I began another new journey. Well, let's call it an extension of the previous journey. At any rate, it is a completely different path than I have found myself on before. I didn't expect to find myself here. In fact, I thought I had already healed. But I obviously had not, because now I can see how emotionally broken I have really been. There has always been a head knowledge. "You're smart. You know this already." I have heard that over and over again. And yes, cognitively I knew, but in my spirit, my heart, my soul, I was still longing for a different answer, a different reality.

I just could not accept that I was where I was.

My emotions—I had never fully dealt with any of them. I have partially; I have jumped around them, I have danced with them, I have pushed through them, and I have swallowed them. I have never truly slowed down long enough to allow myself to *feel* them. Grief, sadness, anger, disappointment, abandonment, and rejection all still reside to some degree inside me. I will unpack them at times and use them in different situations, which is emotionally unhealthy for obvious reasons. I will respond to something inappropriately because what I am really feeling is much deeper than the tiny infraction I am facing. But they have to get out, especially when I'm feeling bad. I have unloaded unearned and unmerited emotions on an unsuspecting person or situation. The punishment doesn't fit the crime, but I justified it by saying, "I am just an emotional person" when I should have been saying, "I am unhealthy in my responses and my emotions."

In all of my studies, I found that the little girl inside had never healed. I hadn't treated myself with the same kindness I could so easily give to others. The longer I ignored the hurt inside, the more I felt compelled to control anything and everyone around me. When I began to lose control, I would react, respond, and just reel out of control. I liked to call this being emotional, when it was really just a temper tantrum in adult form.

Wow. That hit home.

Finally, I am at a place where I can own myself. I can see with my head and feel with my heart the hurt I can cause and have caused by not caring for myself emotionally. I allow myself to feel everything, to absorb it express it, and release it. That is the biggest part: letting it go.

"Let it Go." LOL.

My closest friends like to sing that Disney song to me because they know me so well. Letting go involves trust. It requires belief. It requires having *positive* thoughts and having faith that all things do work together for the good. I struggled with that. Why? Because fear reigned in my heart.

Truly, truly let go of the control, the fear—everything. Fear—fear of failure, fear of rejection, even fear of success—cripples the greatest things. Fear makes us react rather than act. Fear causes us to make decisions that can hurt rather than heal. We have to be brave. We have to be intentional. To experience that which we desire, we have to be different than we've been before.

In the end, it's worth the risk.

1. *What are you afraid of most?*
   Being alone? Failing? Think honestly about this, because it is usually what triggers us to make the wrong decision. Once we know and understand our fears, we can face them more effectively. Mine is being alone. So in order to face that, I make a point of doing things that I love with just myself. I get myself excited about it. I even plan what I'll wear. It is like a date, just with my favorite person—*me*. I sit back and appreciate myself.

2. *What emotions are you avoiding? What triggers you to react rather than act?*
   We all have experienced disappointment, fear, and even rejection. We have to be able to face those emotions without fear. Put them out on the table and put words to why you feel the way you do. There is *no* wrong answer. I keep a journal with me at all times. I take notes—even just a sentence or two—to help me process. You would be shocked to see what you write when you look back a month later.

3. *What do you need to let go of?*
   A person? A memory? An ideal that you can never meet? I think a lot of times for me, I get stuck on a fantasy, or

an unrealistic expectation. Reality ends up really hurting when, if I was just reasonable with myself or someone else, I could actually let things be what they are. I do know this for sure: forcing *anything never works*. When kids play with those shape sorters and shove a round peg into a square hole, it leaves huge gaps, and the space is never full. Do the same to a square peg in a round hole and you end up shaving off parts you never meant to leave.

3
Lying to Myself

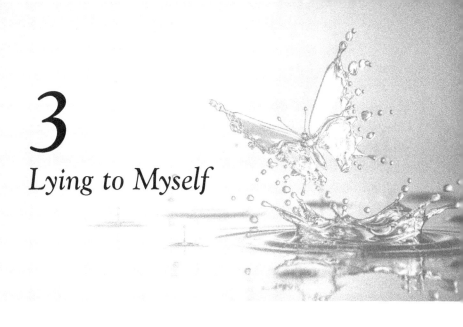

My fear of not being good enough for others became a huge obstacle in my life. It did not matter how often someone would say or even show me they loved and accepted me; my inner demons would not allow me to believe or even accept it as true. I almost ruined one of the most important relationships in my life by doing this, and I injured many others.

People grow weary of constantly being the one to give you validation. They cannot be your source. You have to be able to truly love who you are and care for yourself before you can have a healthy relationship.

Because I never took the time to really deal with my inner self, to learn and grow and heal from old wounds, I began creating new wounds to emphasize my lack of self-worth. Every situation and every relationship would just compound, and my insecurities would grow deeper. I would get angry because I would find myself facing the same situations over and over again.

I even began to see myself as a victim, but in all reality, I was not. I had made the choices to put myself in the positions

I was in. I had neglected myself both physically and emotionally by choosing to ignore the pain I felt inside. I was on this huge merry-go-round of the same emotions but with different faces attached. It had become a pattern, and one I knew I needed to change.

I know that I am not alone in this. I know there are others who struggle with patterns in life. There are things we desperately want to change but fear we never can, things we want to overcome so we can truly learn to love in a healthy relationship, not a toxic one.

I thought I had healed. I thought I had done the work.

But when I found myself running headlong into yet another dysfunctional relationship, I realized I had definitely not. I left my closest friends. They warned me. They knew I was heading for disaster. But I didn't care. I rationalized. I justified. I just wanted it to work.

The signs were all there. Every flag was red—not a green one in the bunch. I was not looking at the flags. I was only looking at the void the relationship filled in my heart. The voices of my friends and family echoed in my ears. Some of them even stepped away from me during this time because I just refused to listen. I was shut off from everyone and everything except the relationship with him. And "him" was any number of guys I had dated. "He" became my world, my everything.

I did this with most of my relationships. I let the guy be my focus, my identity, and the center of my world. No one is meant to fill every part of you.

Far too many times I found myself letting someone else tell me who I needed to be or how I needed to look. It was me giving up control in an effort to be loved and accepted.

Things escalated (as they always do) and I found myself in the cycle of pushing them away and then pulling them back. I was just as much a part of the cycle as they were, if not more. I found myself at times in the bathroom just questioning what the hell I thought I was doing, wondering if this was the life I had worked for. But my heart was for them. I could always see the good in them, deep down. I believed they were hurting and needed love. I believed I could love them like they had never been loved before. I believed they could and would change.

I was lying to myself that I could make a difference, lying to my family about what was really going on, and lying to the men just to keep the peace. I would say I was okay when I wasn't.

I was totally reliving my past every time. This was far worse than anything I had ever known as a child. It was worse because I was allowing it. I was in control and I couldn't stop myself.

Truth sets you free. Truth hurts. Truth requires actions. I was not ready to take action.

Looking back, I believe I had lost my mind. Nothing I did made sense.

Who allows another person to make them feel less than?

Who subjects themselves to constant ridicule and anger?

Who allows their boundaries (if they have any) to be violated again and again without remorse?

The answer is, honestly, a person who has no self-worth, who has allowed other people's voices to drown out their own, who has allowed his or her own self-hate to rule. That had become me. I was that person. I know I am not the only person who has ever allowed abuse. I know I am not alone. There are many women who settle. There are many who are drawn to the chaos. Why? Because of unresolved trauma in our hearts and souls. Because rather than choosing the truth, we choose a lie.

A lie that says,
- This is all you deserve.
- This is the best you can do.
- It will get better.
- I can fix this.
- I created this.

The truth says,
- You deserve love and care.
- You can have the best of life.
- People don't live this way.
- You cannot control another person, for good or bad.

The truth says,
- Be strong. Walk away.
- You are worth it.

It took me many times of lying to myself to finally come to the point where I knew I could walk away. I had health issues that I had to attend to. I believe sometimes God allows things to happen so we have to choose. That is where I found myself. For once, I chose myself over another person.

1. *What lies (that you or someone else has said) do you believe about yourself?*
   Write down all the things you hate about yourself. Then write down the exact opposite of that. For example, for "I am unlovable," write "I *am* lovable"; for "I am unattractive," write "I am perfectly made—every part." Take the list of the lies and burn it. Take the list of the truths and put it near your kitchen sink, on your fridge, or on your bathroom mirror and read it *out loud* to yourself every time you are there! Train your mind to think on the truth, not the lie.

2. *Write down one thing you'd like to change about yourself. Be realistic. Then write down how you can go about making that change. Ask for help from a friend if you have to. But don't just write down what you'd like to change; write down one thing you love about yourself. Again, if you need a friend to help, then ask! We all have strengths and weaknesses. That is what makes us human.*

4
The Decision

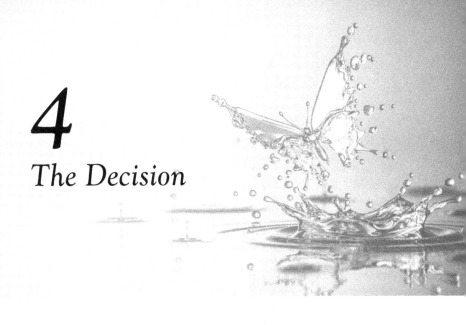

I was at a crossroads each time. I knew that I knew what I needed to do. But I continued to question myself. I called my friends. They would no longer talk with me about it. They had been there through it all before and were tired. They said I knew what I needed to do. They would no longer entertain me and my longing for affirmation. They considered it enabling me. So, I was left to do some serious soul searching.

Here is what I discovered:

1. **You only ask when you *already* know.**

    What I mean is this: you know in your gut what is best for you. You only ask others because you want validation in your choice; you want someone to affirm what you have decided. I am not saying to not seek advice. It is said there is wisdom in a multitude of counselors, *but* only if you are willing to really listen, and only if you are ready for a perspective you do not necessarily like. You must *know* yourself and trust yourself. Honor yourself and your opinion more than any others because only you live your life. Also know they can see things you are sometimes blind to because you are in the middle of it.

What is that saying, "You can't see the forest through the trees?"

My friend Beth used to say I was guilty of being an "askhole." What she meant by that is this: "Do not ask me a question just to ignore it and do your own thing." She knew me very well. She knew my stubborn ways; I would ask her opinion but already know what I was going to do. I was going through the motions. It was lip service only. It was a façade. Nothing would change; I would just have the appearance of desiring to change. And she was not going to play the game with me. She would not validate my poor choices or waste her time if I didn't seriously want to change.

If you are going to really change your situations, you must get out of your own way. You must be willing to do something new. It will be uncomfortable. It may even be painful. But I guarantee you, it will be worth it. *You* are worth it.

When we choose not to address our own hurts, or not deal with our issues, but instead cover them with a relationship, we cheat ourselves out of an authentic life. We become a character in a story, a story that is not and cannot be a reality. It just isn't possible.

When we ask our friends for their opinions only to justify our actions, when we already know the truth but want a different answer, we are cheating ourselves. We are attempting to validate our actions when we know deep down that they are wrong.

We must find the truth within. We must look deeper. We must be bold. It takes more courage to face than to ignore ourselves. It is scary to truly see our insecurities. It is difficult to own our part in the devastation we find ourselves in. But if we are to grow, to change, to become healthy, and to break the cycle, it is required.

2. If you commit to yourself the way you commit to others, you *will* love yourself again.

> This is a big one for me. I never truly loved myself. So how could I honestly believe anyone else really loved me?
>
> Some of us cannot imagine liking ourselves, let alone loving ourselves. It takes intention. It takes spending time on you. It takes making your needs a priority.
>
> But in order to make your needs a priority, you have to know what they are!
>
> Write them out. Know what they are. Commit them to memory. Commit to yourself to not violate them under *any* circumstances, for *any* hope of a reward.
>
> I was guilty of this. I would give and give until I was completely bankrupt emotionally, mentally, physically, and even financially at times.
>
> I would abandon my wants or desires in an effort to fill theirs. If they were fulfilled, they wouldn't

have time to notice my inadequacy. Rather than working on bettering who I was so I could *overcome* my inadequacy, I would cover it with acts of service or kindness to others.

I became a master at it. I would go to work, run around all afternoon doing errands for others and ignoring my own needs. I never took the time to invest in myself—physically, emotionally, and even financially. I would drain my bank account, I would bankrupt my emotions, I would ignore my physical needs—all in an effort to be loved. Their love would define me. It would prove my worth. But it never did. What it did was magnify my weakness. This is such a tragedy.

When I finally decided to try taking a chance on myself, I started small. I committed to just thirty minutes every day for me alone. If that was riding a bike, great. If it was reading a book, even better. If it was just simply meditating, whatever form it was, I made a promise to myself to just do it.

I began doing things like investing in a yoga instructor, a wellness coach, and a vision board program. These were things I put off because I said I didn't have the time or money. I really did—I just chose not to. I began to focus on what I like, what I want, and what I need. It felt very selfish at first. And there were times (I'm not going to lie) that I would cry that what I *wanted* was a person to love me!

I felt so helpless, so overwhelmed. But I continued on the path. I knew I had to try something different than what I had in the past. *When you keep finding yourself in the same situations over and over, it is time to change course even if it is uncomfortable.*

When I began liking myself and doing things that made me feel good about *me*, I was a better person. I was less insecure. I became stronger. In turn, I began to be happier. The peace I was looking for was within the entire time.

3. If you want to change, do it for you alone, *not* anyone else.

Constantly seeking validation from others is only a temporary fix. People change, relationships change, and situations change. You will never arrive at peace; you will never have solid footing because it is ever changing. The only solid thing in your life is you. *You* are the constant, so *you* decide what needs to be in your life, what your goals and your dreams are, and so on.

Do not give someone else the power to define you. Do not look to them to be your identity. You are who you are. Before they ever came into your life, you were you. When or if they leave, you will still be you. If you have things you struggle with about yourself, that is a personal matter. It is not something you are required to share, unless of course you want to, or you are in a healthy relationship where there is support and encouragement not shaming or ridicule. It is *never* okay for someone you love to make you feel less than. *Read that again.*

It is *not* love to put someone down, call the person names, or yell at or ridicule—it is control. It is manipulation. It is wrong, regardless of the circumstances. If the person does not respect you or your feelings enough to be encouraging and supportive, or if he or she finds you do not meet his or her standards, the other person can simply find someone else. There are over a billion people in this world. The other person *is not* your person, no matter how badly you want him or her to be. Let the person go.

4. People are happier when they aren't lying to themselves.
I lied to myself. I lied to everyone around me as well. I said things were fine, that I was okay. I said love involves sacrifice. But what I did not allow for was for the sacrifice to be on both sides, not just on my side.

Lying to yourself takes on many forms.

- It can be saying everything is ok when you are dying inside.
- It can be making excuses for the abuse you are living with.
- It can be agreeing with the awful things that are said about you.
- It can be pretending you like certain things that really bother you deep inside.
- It can be denying your beliefs in order to appease others.

Whatever the form, it is destructive. It will kill your spirit. It will drain your emotions. It will destroy your future.

Be real. Be honest with yourself. Find your truth, whatever that may be. It can be simple. My truth is that I am okay. I am not a quitter. I will fail a thousand times, but I *will* keep going. I will love wholly, even if it hurts in the end and I lose. At least I know I showed up. I can't get mad at myself for that. I must be true to who I am. I used to get angry when a relationship was lost. I thought it was my failure, but that is *not* true. Failure would have been if I never tried, if I never opened myself up. Because my heart is meant to love. And I'm living a lie if I don't pursue that wholeheartedly.

Find your truth. Know yourself. Commit to who you truly are, and only change what you want to.

Live for the present, because this is all we have. But please keep hoping for the future, rather than looking at your past. If you keep looking at your past, you will only stay stuck. You will repeat the same thing over and over. My dear friend Paul advises me (almost) daily that you cannot enjoy your present or build a future when you keep bringing up the past. You cheat yourself of ever having the happiness you desire. Do not continue to waste your time. Just let it go. Forgive yourself. Move on.

Paul is the epitome of strength and courage. He works tirelessly in his self-owned business. He has been my example of what true love looks like. He may not be perfect, but he is constant. He is reliable. Most of all, he is kind. I have come to understand that our true friends do not always tell us what we want to hear. They can say things that even hurt, but it is because they have our best interests at heart. They want to see us succeed. One thing I can count on Paul for is that he will not enable me to stay the same. If I am in a bad frame of mind, he will correct me—with love, of course. But he doesn't just correct me—he stays by my side to help me see it through. I am so grateful for him in my life. We all have a Paul. We all have someone we can go to for a perspective on our situation. Some of us are fortunate enough to have many Pauls. If you feel you do not, I challenge you to sit down and think of all the people you have in your life. You may be surprised at who has been there the whole time, and you just did not notice them for who they were.

Find your people. Surround yourself with them. Because when you do, you can't help but change. You can't help but grow. But you have to be willing to do the work. And it isn't always easy.

1. *Who is your Paul? Who is there for you anytime, anywhere, no questions asked. Write that person a thank you note. Let him or her know how much he or she impacts your life. Show gratitude. Be a Paul for someone else!*

2. *Be a Paul to yourself as well. Be your own best advocate.*

5
The Escape

Dig deeper.

    I made the choice to leave. I decided I could not live the life I was living. I handed back the keys and left. I knew what I was doing. I knew it could not continue. Yet, it hurt like hell to do. It still hurts to this day.

    If I knew it was bad for me, why was it so very difficult to let go?

    Because I had hoped for a life together. I invested my heart in it. I purchased things for our dream. I pushed the relationship away when things happened I could not handle, when my emotions had hit their limit, when my heart hurt so badly I would cry at work, and when I realized I would be alone—again. I was fulfilling my self-prophecy of not being worthy. I would pull the relationship back to myself. It really was crazy. It was unbelievable, yet I was guilty.

    There was so much that was unresolved. And I think I almost liked it that way, because it gave me hope. Hope of what? Hope that we could one day be together, just the way I dreamed. I had this story in my head of what could be. It was nowhere near what truly was, but I could make myself believe it. I could take the brief moments of kindness and hold onto them for dear life, like a toddler grips a dirty piece of candy the child's mom is trying to rip from his or her hands. It was bad for me, yet I refused to let go completely.

I could overlook the despair I would feel when I knew they hated the very sight of my body. It was repulsive. I was told over and over again how unattractive I was. Other girls would get compliments while I watched.

I could repress all my feelings of insufficiency and push myself to be better, to be acceptable.

But I finally got to a time that was different. I decided to let go of the control. I decided I *had* to change. I *had to* just really let it all go: all hopes, all dreams, all wishes.

I let go—but didn't at the same time.

At first, I had little check marks indicating that if something happened, it was either a sign that we still had a chance or that they were moving on.

Obviously, I loved the little indicators that I could have them back. Maybe they missed me? Maybe they would come back?

And the signs that they were moving on, well, they devastated me. It was like I wanted to torture myself, like I needed the pain in order to matter. So wrong.

I had let them be my identity. I let them tell me my worth. I allowed them to say whatever they felt, and I agreed with it, even if it cut me to the very core. I did this because I desired acceptance. I craved knowing I fit somewhere, even if that somewhere was toxic to me.

Even in their absence, I was letting the relationship define me.

If they looked at my social media, then they still cared. If they liked another girl's post, then they had moved on. Absolutely ridiculous. It was childlike, but there I was just engaging in all of the turmoil. I was asking for it. I couldn't get enough. And the craziest part is that I am the one who left. It made absolutely no sense at all.

I failed. I manipulated (tried doing certain things in hopes the relationship would get better). I tried forcing something I should have walked away from at the very beginning. I knew then that it would not last. But I forged ahead, with no regard for the red flags. There were many moments I would find myself in the bathroom, just looking at my reflection asking myself, "What the hell are you doing here?" This is not the life I wanted. I walked on eggshells. I pretended much of the time that all was well, when I knew deep down it was not.

The back and forth in my heart was heavy. It was constant, but I had finally made the decision and was not going to waver. I may get tired. I may get scared, but I will keep moving—for myself.

The journey had begun.

I finally made the decision for myself. I felt confident and bold. I had lined things up to have success. I was a little sad to be honest. But how long had it been since I had been truly happy? I wanted every relationship to be different. I wanted it to be mine forever. In my heart I really knew this was not possible, but I refused to see the truth and told myself a lie instead. I made excuses for the bad behavior. I tried forgetting the cruel words. I pushed forward—covered, buried, hid—whatever was necessary to keep the fantasy alive.

Time, it's all about time. Time and waiting. Time and waiting and patience. Relationships take time—a lot of it. I have been guilty of rushing in. I have been guilty of chasing the relationship rather than just letting it evolve (if it is even meant to), and inadvertently causing it to blow up in my face.

Is it good to rush and hurry and maneuver just to try to keep a volatile heart steady? Is putting the stress and weight of someone else's peace on your own shoulders good? I wanted so badly to hold those brief few moments of bliss in my heart and overlook the obvious unhappiness that surrounded not just me but them as well.

A friend said to me, "We all like to think we can change someone by our good heart or attitude, but far too often the one trying to elevate another ends up falling into an abyss of sadness." I feel this very deeply.

I wanted to be enough, to be desired, to be loved, in all of these relationships, o be snuggled and cared for—hell, even just talked to with kindness. But that was not to be had. Instead, I was accused, criticized, and made to feel like a child. I questioned everything about myself. I searched within to find acceptance and encouragement—but I grew so tired. This happened over and over again. The pattern was clear.

I wanted to give up. I wanted to crawl into a hole and never come out. I could not face those who had warned me this would happen. I was so stubborn. I had been here before. My other relationships had huge red flags. I ignored those as well. I lost friends over my relationships with them. I was so desperate to find and know love that I sacrificed what was right in front of me: the true love of friends.

I felt incomplete without a man to define me. I did not think I was enough to define myself. So, here I stood again in the same situation, only I had alienated myself from everyone who loved me. I was thousands of miles from the refuge and safety of my true friends.

I left true love for a lie. What I had failed to recognize was that love, the kind I was looking for, had been with me all along: the love of my children. They not only accepted me—they supported me.

I left the love of my friends, friends who only wanted the best for me, who were there trying to save me from myself—yet I wouldn't let them.

I left the love of my family, who desperately wanted me to see my worth, to know my value was in myself not in another, as I had thought.

I was so busy looking at what I thought I did not have; I could not clearly see what I did.

When I finally made the move to leave, while it was very difficult, I could start to see clearly. Sure, there were moments of despair, of sadness, and of regret. But in the end, I knew I was better off.

Sometimes deciding who you are is deciding who you will never be again. That is what I did.

No matter the confusion or fear, I made a choice to stay the course.

1. *Who do you want to be? Define yourself. How will you get there? What is in your way?*
   Get out of your head. You can be anything you want to be.

2. *What things do you have in your life (such as people, your job, your children, or your health) that you take for granted?*
   Write a list. Every day thank God or the Universe for giving you those things because they *are* gifts. We are not entitled to anything in this life.

6
The Freedom

Weeks into my healing, I had been intentional in doing things for myself. It was a strange feeling, picking only the very best for myself. But I was trying. I visited a really cool store here and this is how it went:

Standing at the seafood counter trying to decide what fish I wanted to cook for myself for dinner, I spotted Chilean sea bass at $28.99 per pound. My eyes lit up, because on all the cooking shows I had watched, they always talked about what an amazing fish it is. I had always wanted to try it. I took in the whole case of seafood. I finally landed on tilapia for $7.99 per pound—not even close to the sea bass in taste or quality. If I had been thinking of making dinner for someone else, I wouldn't have considered anything other than the very best. Why was it so hard for me to want to do for myself that which I found so easy to do for another? What was the disconnect? And was I the only one who struggled with this? I pondered this while I told the man behind the counter to add a filet of the sea bass to my order. He obliged, and I felt a foot taller knowing I had done something special for myself. I walked out with my treasure and a sparkle in my eyes. I was full of anticipation and expectation.

I am currently in the process of learning to love myself the way I love others. I am guilty of investing far more in another person than in my own wellbeing. These are simple things, like buying myself something I like, not just what the others like, creating an event centered entirely around their passions or desires and forgetting who I am in the process, or taking more time to accomplish an errand for them while putting what I need done on hold. I completely forgot who I was, or what I wanted, or needed. I called it love because it was. But it was also self-sabotage.

Why? Because it has nothing to do with the one you are trying to love—not at all. It has everything to do with how you love yourself. In my heart, I desired to prove my love by my sacrifice. But in my head, I was telling myself I wasn't as important. My actions and decisions were never about me, and my spirit knew it. I broke myself down. And the ones I tried loving, well, they knew I loved them, but they could see plainly how little I loved myself. And in that, they lost for me what I was trying so desperately for: reciprocation of love, honor, and respect. I never truly understood that I had to put myself first at times in order to care for myself well. You have to care for yourself in order to adequately care for others. It is not selfish. It is self-full. Yes, I made up a word.

I am finally understanding I have to look within for what I need, what I desire, what I want. I have to see myself, truly see myself for me. I have to appreciate and evolve into the woman I desire to be. No one else can do it for me. All the acceptance and love of another will never ever be enough. It has to come from within. You cannot find validation from another.

Reset

1. *Self-care is so much more than fancy nails, hair extensions, or even sea bass. What do you do to make yourself a priority? What changes do you need to make? Saying no can be self-care. Setting boundaries is self-care. You are worth it.*

2. *How can you invest in you?*
   Start that side hustle. Join that class. Pay for a coach. Do something that helps you become a better version of yourself.

7
The Present

Today I sit with myself and know that I am okay.

I get to walk on the beach whenever I want to.

My children are all healthy.

I have a good home.

I have a good job.

I have good friends—even if they are busy.

I do not feel like I am lacking in any area.

I am loved.

I am not quite where I want to be, but I feel that I am so very close.

I do not feel lonely.

I don't feel like I am missing anything.

I am content to just sit—sit and absorb, sit and rest, sit and be.

In the past, I would run to and fro. I was known as the girl who wanted it done yesterday. I had no patience. If things did not move quickly enough, well, then I would move them myself. This was not just in relationships. This was in every single area of my life. It is a frustrating way to live for sure. It causes you to question, it causes you to create drama where there is none, it causes you to want to give up. *Why?* Because life is not about forcing things.

Life is about living. Living is *now*. Living is just simply breathing in and out, in and out.

When you take the time to really do this, your perspective changes. You get the full view rather than the one thing you have been focusing or obsessing over. I have a friend, Kyle, who helps me see things differently. He will sit for hours with me and ask questions. He will even frustrate me at times with all of the questions. He does this so I will see things in a different way. He does this sometimes to shake me intellectually. We have some pretty heated discussions that always end well. It doesn't mean I always agree with him, but it means that I can acknowledge a different (and at times a much needed) view.

One thing he always tells me is that just because I see something a certain way or would do it a certain way does not make another person's way wrong. Please read that again. I believe a lot of us get stuck or fixated on our view, our way, our desires. Being stuck takes us out of the present because we are not accepting the present.

I learned that the things or people or relationships we obsess over are usually related to an unhealed trauma in our hearts. It's like we want to go back and have a do-over. We have to be able to just accept. We have to absorb the now.

I am not saying do not hope for change. I am not saying to give up on dreams. I am saying to live today. Do not get lost in the past hurts that cause you to fear what the future is and ruin what is right now. I hope that makes sense. It all comes back to seeing what truly is—not what we want or what we fear, but what actually is truth.

I found that I have the love I have been searching for. It may not look the way I had imagined it. I have my children who not only love me, but like me as well. I have the unmoving love of friends who sit tirelessly with me while I make mistake after mistake. They stay by my side and encourage me to be better. Most of all, the most important love I now possess is the love of myself—the acceptance of myself.

For years I chased love. I fixated on it, almost obsessed over it. I cried about it, created drama over it. I would force things. I would even manipulate. I hate to admit that but if we are being transparent, I must. I was totally missing the fact that what I was looking for I already had. I was looking for acceptance. I was looking for inclusion. I was looking for peace. I was looking for myself.

I needed to show up for myself for once. I needed to prove to myself I cared for me. I needed to do the self-care that truly mattered: saying no, setting boundaries, valuing my heart more than another's—the true self care of taking the time to work on me.

I had spent my entire life avoiding myself. I was so focused on others and their demons so I would not have to see or face my own. I know I am not the only one who has done this. It is the biggest reason we get into toxic relationships; we can focus on what they need to fix rather than fixing ourselves. Yes, I said it. We can blame the person we are in the toxic relationship with for their bad behavior, we can call ourselves victims. But if we get real with ourselves, we are just as much to blame for not showing up for ourselves. We are the ones who allow the toxicity in our lives. We choose not to believe we have the power to change. We choose to believe we deserve this and that we cannot have better. Now this is *not* to say an abuser has the right to harm us; I am saying that if we see the red flags, know they are present, and yet continue on, we have to take accountability for that.

We have to *get out*—period. No excuses. No bargaining. No delays. As my good friend Molly would say, "Get the f*** out." It doesn't get any clearer than that. But sometimes we get so used to the drama and mistreatment that it is more comfortable to stay than to leave. This is where I found myself, repeatedly, not just in romantic relationships but work ones as well. I would run around working overtime, killing myself just to prove I was worth having.

I know what I am saying can be seen as controversial. Some may interpret it that I am advocating for the abuser. I am not at all. I am speaking to myself. There was a complete abandonment of myself, and not in the healthy way. I abandoned caring about what harm could come to me in order to have the presence of a man in my life. I sacrificed my very well being to feel "love" or acceptance. There were nights I would go to bed and not know what I would wake up to.

There were nights I *would* wake up to the lights being turned on and someone standing over my bed just glaring at me. Then the yelling would start, the intimidation, then the walking out and making me feel like I should not close my eyes again. I could see the possibility of the danger. I abandoned my basic human needs for what I thought I needed: a partner. I had chosen this. I stopped being a victim to him and became a victim to myself and my toxic unhealed heart.

1. *What are your absolutes in life? Write them down. Your non-negotiables? Read them daily. These are your red flags when someone shows you who they are. A red flag for you may not be a red flag for another. Don't judge your list. Be honest with yourself about what you can and can't live with. Then don't betray yourself by ignoring it.*

2. *What do you obsess about? Write it down. Why does it consume you? Is there unresolved hurt regarding that? I found that I was obsessed with rejection. I had a negative view on what it meant. I had to dig deeper and discover that it was not about me, it was all about the other people: their likes, their needs, their wants. Taking the responsibility off myself helps me accept that rejection is actually a gift because I don't have to perform anymore. I can just be me, and the right ones come into my life while the wrong ones leave. It is a gift to be thankful for something to not control me.*

8
If-Then Bullshit

This is going to make a lot of people mad, but I am sick and tired of hearing about "name it, claim it," about manifesting what you want, and it will magically appear.

I went to a church for a long time, and the church members stood firm in their belief that whatever you spoke, you would receive. They also believed that scripture stated very specifically God's promises were all like a math equation. *If* you do this, *then* God will do that. Imagine if you can, how much I felt like I failed when my marriage fell apart, despite all my words and all my math equations of trying to get God to move on our behalf. I was devastated. I was angry, which was just covering my shame and pain.

Living under that belief and trying to fix my life doing everything I was told, just to watch it in shambles, I became so disillusioned and so depressed. And it was entirely wrong teaching, because there were two people involved, not just me! God couldn't make my husband change no matter how many rules I followed to get one of His promises! I could only allow God to change me. Focus on me.

I had to do the work for change—but only on myself.

Later I encountered a friend who sincerely believed in manifestation. She gave me all these instructions on writing down what I want, speaking it over and over, and then eventually burning it under a new moon. She insisted that if I did that, the universe would bring me everything I wanted.

Sounds similar, doesn't it?

But the funny thing is that it didn't work either. And I wondered to myself, if either belief were true, wouldn't *we all* have everything we want? No one would be sick. No one would be homeless. No one would be lovesick over someone.

No. I do *not* believe we can speak our future into being. I do *not* believe we can think or send vibes into the universe and get back all we dream. However, if I haven't lost you yet in your anger towards my words, I *do* believe we get what we want by hard work. Hard work involves thinking correctly. Hard work requires speaking to yourself with the right words. Hard work asks for effort, not just sitting.

So, in some ways, both of the teachings I have experienced have a certain element of truth.

Here is the balance of the two.

Recently, I purchased my dream vehicle: a Jeep. I was so excited because I just love the feel of riding with the doors off and the wind blowing my hair into a mess. What better place to do this than the beach.

I got the Jeep home and found it had some things wrong with it. When I took it back to the dealer, they tried fixing it numerous times to no avail. I finally ended up returning it and going back to my hated compact car that looks like a grandma car. (Forget that I *am* a grandma! I don't want to look like one!) Every time I got in that car, I told myself, "My car does not define me. My car does not define me."

Well, just last week I found another Jeep that I liked even more than the last. It was my favorite color and everything. I decided to take a chance on it. It turns out it was a hard no. The price was just not where it needed to be and there were some concerns about the vehicle I wanted to trade towards it. I graciously said, "Okay, thank you anyway," and left with no other thoughts of the Jeep.

Well, that isn't entirely true. I did think when I saw others driving around that I still wanted one for myself. That want stayed in my heart, but I didn't let it rule me. A few days later, I received a call from the sales guy who was helping me. He said, "I am so sorry to bother you on a Sunday. I was so excited to talk to you. Is now a good time?"

I said yes.

He went on to excitedly tell me how he had been working on this since I left the dealership, and how he was able to work an incredible deal for me. I was blown away. They offered to take the vehicle in question at more value than it was worth, give me every insurance possible, all the bells and whistles, and keep the price right where I wanted to be.

I could hardly believe it. It was such a gift—a better one than I had even dreamed of.

I think if we can believe, ask, and learn to receive, we will live a better life. What I mean by that is we should not try to control the outcome of our asking.

I am so guilty of this.

I think I want something a certain way, when in reality, I think too small. I put it into my box when it needs to be in a moving van holding the smallness of my box. We limit ourselves. We see things in part and we get stuck.

All of this applies to loving yourself. It isn't automatic. It's not a quick fix. It has to be intentional.

To love yourself is not easy because it's too easy to compare yourself to others. It's too easy to hear others' voices in your head. It's too easy to buy into the belief you're not lovable because you've tried relationship after relationship only to have heartbreak upon heartbreak. Loving yourself requires much work. But the good news is you *can* do it. It may not be immediate, it will be uncomfortable at times, but it can be done.

Remember: believe, ask, receive.
- Believe in yourself.
- Ask yourself the hard questions. Do the work.
- Receive the gift.

Remember, when you do this, the gift may not come the way you envision. You may want to look like Barbie when you should look like Mary Lou Retton. You get the idea.

An example of this for me is working out. When I was much younger and before I had children, I was a gymnast and loved riding my bike. But I haven't actively done much physical activity in the past few years due to putting everyone and everything in front of working out. In fact, I just didn't believe I could get back into anything again. When I tried with a trainer, I only saw it as punishing my body for not being good enough. But boy howdy, I was going to force myself into working out, come hell or high water! I would go strong for a brief period of time and then quit because I didn't get the same results as all the girls I saw around me. I was on a constant rollercoaster of emotions—until just recently.

My life changed drastically. And I had no choice but to put myself and my body first.

I had to find a way to finally step into my own self in order to become who I am. It was painful at times to see my failures, to know that I was choosing this life. But it was necessary in order for me to truly heal and to become the best version of myself. I took up yoga. I learned how my mind and body work can together, not fight each other. For years, my mind hated my body. And I believe my body responded. I had terrible indigestion, to the point of throwing up. I grew lesions in my throat. My body knew I hated it. And I believe it gave me back all the negativity I was putting into it.

I never wanted to work out because it was already a reminder to me of what I wasn't: I was not tall and thin. I didn't have gorgeous legs. My arms were not perfectly toned, and I looked awful in the mirror (that they have *everywhere* in a gym; I am sure they are meant to encourage people, but they just compounded my inadequacy). I could never focus on what I was good at when at the gym. I was too busy seeing what I could never be. So working out was a torture session rather than a celebration of what my body was. Even if it was something I enjoyed, like bicycling, I would focus on how clunky I thought I was. I was sure everyone was looking at me laughing at my huge thighs in shorts. In fact, for years I refused to wear shorts of any kind.

I was telling myself how unworthy I was, how unlovable. I would use exercise as punishment, pushing myself to the point of hurting. It was my penance for being so gross.

With every repetition and every set, I would under my breath say how gross I was, how I deserved to hurt because I was not good enough. I never once reveled in the fact that my stocky legs could squat 180 pounds or bike for over twenty miles. I never appreciated that I was flexible enough to put my feet completely behind my head. I was just so consumed with what I thought I needed to be in order to be truly loved, I couldn't open myself up to the knowledge that I was worthy just because I was me.

My boyfriends compounded my feeling of body shaming. They would tell me how I was the heaviest girlfriend ever, how I was unattractive, and that I couldn't possibly be overweight forever. In fact, one time I was on a trip and I was told he was not attracted to me. I crawled into bed in a gross, unsightly manner. It devastated me. I had opened my heart up to love, to the very possibility of a relationship, again and again. I had been very real about who I was.

I made myself vulnerable. I would share photos with my flaws plainly visible. I was broken down, told that I could maybe one day become a goddess. I was assured I had a pretty face. I was told that if you only looked at my face, you could get over my physique.

I let them define me. I let them say those things. Why? Because deep down I believed them. Deep down, I agreed I was only worthy of love if I looked perfect. I was convinced this was why love had evaded me my entire life. So, I decided I *had* to do something. I thought, *Well, what have you not done?* Yoga came to mind. I had been told it was a good stress reliever as well. I could definitely use that! I went to the internet to find my class. I would change. I would become better. I would become worthy. I found one. I was excited. I signed up for the following Saturday.

When I began my journey with yoga, it was, of all places, on the beach. It was a small group of women, maybe five at best. My yoga instructor, of course, was this waif of a girl who I could only dream of being. She was practically perfect in every way. And the other women had all been there before in their cute little yoga wear. I was only in my shorts and tank top. I was intimidated for sure! What was I even thinking? The beach? An audience? I didn't even know what a downward dog was. But there I was, doing it anyway.

I told myself that I would do the entire class—no backing out. Casey was the instructor's name. She was good. She was kind. She made sure to let everyone know to do what she could. There was no right or wrong in yoga. *Yeah right*, I thought to myself. I was sure everyone was inwardly chuckling at this overweight woman in her poses. But I kept going. I was told to focus on my breath. And I found the more I focused on my breath, the less I could focus on the negative thoughts trying to invade my mind.

I never knew there was a better way to breathe. I liked it. It felt good. It felt right. I kept going.

When the class was over, Casey came over to tell me that I had perfectly maneuvered each pose. She went on to say how impressed she was with my form. I was so excited to find that

I could do this. I wanted to hire her on a weekly basis to keep the accountability going. And for the first time I actually looked forward to exercising. I did not dread it. I knew it would stretch me. I knew it would challenge me. But I knew if I kept going, and kept breathing, I could do it.

One thing I found was that yoga is a balance of effort and ease, just as life is. You do the work, and the work makes a way for you. But you *have* to do the work. Change cannot happen without it. I have used yoga in my everyday life. It has changed me. Whenever I find things to be overwhelming—traffic for example—I just stop and breathe. If I am in a stressful situation and I feel the urge to fight or flight, I stop and focus on my breathing: slow, deliberate, steady, cleansing, calming. I have learned to become intentional in everything and not go into auto mode of just going through the actions.

I have also found that yoga has helped me gain perspective on myself. My mind and body work together now. I listen to my body. I care for my body. I challenge my body. But most of all, I celebrate my body and all that it *is*, rather than what it is not. This body grew five beautiful children. This body endured years of abuse. This body was a gift. I had all moving and working limbs. There was so much I had taken for granted. I was a selfish, self-absorbed, ungrateful person, and I longed to change that.

Casey and I agreed while the actual workouts were needed, there were deeper things inside that had to be addressed. My inner child was broken. She had been abandoned long ago. And I had to focus on healing her in order to grow emotionally, physically, mentally, and spiritually. If we do not address all parts of who we are, we will never be completely healthy.

One of my homework assignments with Casey was being honest with myself about the people I had been in relationships with and how they impacted my body image. Here is what I wrote. It is raw. It is harsh. But it is real, and that is all I desire to be. I believe sometimes you have to shock yourself with the cold hard reality instead of the lies you have chosen to accept.

> Your boobs are too big.
> Your stomach is too flabby.
> You have a fat neck.
> There is no need for your legs to be so thick.
> Your feet are short and stubby.
> Check. Check. Check. Check. And check.
> A list of everything I need to change.

It's like the *Frankenstein* movie in my head. I am picturing removing this part, eliminating that part, putting in different pieces, and hiding what flaws I can't change, just to be acceptable in the eyes of another. But then if I do that, what is left of me?

My eyes—the only things that are beautiful, the parts of me that have to watch this disassembling of myself, the windows to my soul. Well, I am afraid my eyes tell a story of disappointment, sadness, and rejection. They have become cloudy and disillusioned with life. They have become tired and sore from the tears I have shed.

Sure, the body is just a shell. Who we are is our heart and soul. But why then can I not be seen for who I am rather than how I look? Why do I have to live my life on your terms? If I am so unattractive and repulsive, then why don't you just leave? No one is forcing you to stay. Please give me my peace back. Please stop taking my self-esteem.

There are over a billion people in this world. Why waste time trying to please the one in front of you and killing yourself slowly with their disapproval, when the other person should be the one encouraging you, loving you, and accepting every part of who you are?

Acceptance does not necessarily mean approval. It does not mean you like something. Acceptance simply means you accept it. You don't focus on the negative. You overlook the flaws. Acceptance means you don't constantly bring it up. Acceptance in its truest form says, "I love you for what you are *and* for what you are *not*."

When I shared this with Casey, she encouraged me to really read and absorb what I wrote. We did some exercises to enforce the opposite of what I was expected to believe about myself. I wrote out the good. I kept the list by my kitchen sink. I would rehearse the good. I would affirm myself. At first, it felt weird. It felt unnatural and forced. But over time, I did gain confidence. I did begin to see the things I wrote as true. When you make room for good, you take away the power of the negative.

Soon after my yoga experience, I decided to incorporate regular workouts at a gym. The first few times, of course, I fought myself. I heard the voices. Mine was the loudest: the voice of self-doubt, the voice of fear of failure. It wasn't until I literally learned to shut my mind off, focus on my breathing, and allow my body to do what it already *knew to do* that I was able to actually complete an hour-long workout. Sure, there were times when it got uncomfortable. But I just would close my eyes, put my thoughts towards my breath, and keep going.

This is the first time in years I have successfully kept up a routine of working out. I don't make excuses. No, I don't always feel it at the time. But when it's over I'm so glad I did it.

My focus changed from forcing my body into submission to celebrating what it could do for me. I became grateful for my strong thick legs, my solid core (yes, stomach) that gave me balance, and my arms that I can literally put anywhere because of my flexibility. I may not see huge rapid change, and neither may anyone else. But the point is *it isn't* about that! It's about me loving me.

1. *Self-care is taking care of your physical body. What do you find to help you? Find something you enjoy not dread. Set aside fifteen minutes every day. Be intentional. Find a buddy if you need accountability, although I find it far more rewarding to just meet myself in the morning. It is more personal and I need that. But that is just me. Do what you need to do so that you can keep your body moving.*

2. *We grow stronger through resistance. None of us likes it but our muscles do not become stronger without it. Learn to lean into the difficult. Find a take-away from it. Know that you grow in the process. What things are challenging you right now? What can you do to lean into them? To learn from them? What is your take-away?*

9
The Healing

Healing from the cycle is hard. It can be exhausting, but it is always worth it. In the end, you win. Know that.

There were many days when I wanted to give up and give in. I wanted to go back to what I knew. It was comfortable. But I did not this time. This time was different.

After a full day of work, running errands, and tidying up my new place, I finally grab the lighter and the candle I just purchased. I take off the lid and smell the sweet floral sunshine in a jar and smiled. I lit it. And then, I proceed to snuggle into my favorite chair by the window with the blanket my mom had made for me at Christmas. It is a special blanket because it has photos of me with all my children on one side and a furry, soft, comforting material on the other side. I have finally settled.

I am making a point, being intentional to sit and allow myself to feel. I realize how I have used things in life to numb the pain. I have stayed busy so I did not have to face the grief I held inside. But now it is time, whether I feel strong enough or not. It is finally time for me to not just face but also embrace that which has held me captive for so long. I have become a master at hiding the pain—or at least in my mind I think I have. But those who are close to me can see. They know. It comes out in the rash decisions I make, or the quick, ugly words that escape from my lips, or the poor life choices I make, when I know better.

But now in the quietness of my home, in my safe place, I am ready. I have my pen and pad in hand. But I set it down for the moment and just reflect. What comes next is almost indescribable. It is a wave, strong and abrupt. I hear the cries of sadness, grief, and utter despair in my belly. I feel it rise from within and it emerges up, up, up my throat and forces itself out of my mouth. Hot tears flood from my eyes, almost stinging my cheeks, like they had been boiling for years just waiting to erupt. And that is exactly what they did. At this point, I am sobbing uncontrollably. I feel the weight of disappointment, regret, sorrow, anger, frustration. I feel it all. I have been running from it for so long, but it finally is free to catch up. I have finally allowed it to overtake every single part of me.

I stayed this way for what seemed like hours, allowing the images of faces—those I have hurt and those who have hurt me—into my thoughts. Watching scenes play out of time, I felt so helpless, so out of control. I never wanted to be weak. I never wanted to be a burden. I never sought out to hurt anyone or anything. But I know I have, all because I could not face myself. I could not allow myself to truly feel. No, I had to be strong. I had to put on my smiling face and do what was necessary. I stayed busy with friends, worked too much, served, volunteered—you name it. I had made myself into superwoman. I had built armor around not just my heart but my soul. The place where I truly feel is the most intimate part of me was a fortress. But all of the things I had tried to keep inside ended up eventually also keeping people out.

So, this is what it means to feel. My skin was like those warm fuzzies we used to give out as kids—you know, the cotton balls with all the prickly things? I was absorbing it; I felt every sensation possible. I hadn't even written down anything. I hadn't made a plan for healing—LOL. But I knew within that I had become stronger at that moment. Something was different. There was a peace, a knowing, a calm, a certainty…of what? Well, that I was going to be okay. I was surrounded by those I love and who love me, literally in my blanket of my babies. And if they could love me when I was spiraling out of control and pushing them away, I knew they would be there to help support me in my newfound freedom of feeling. I didn't have to be ashamed of my failures, because they weren't really failures as I had seen them. Failure is when you don't learn. No, these were life lessons.

I learned that the most beautiful thing in life is that it isn't perfect. I am a mess. And the messes are what makes life beautiful.

I am retraining my mind—what I think about, how I see things, what I focus my time, energy, and heart on. I have a friend who uses the term "center yourself." To me, that means find your balance.

Find the innermost core of who you are, and go there, away from the noise of others, away from the expectations you have for the situation.

Go to the very core of who *you* are, then look at the situation—from inside not outside. When I focus on myself and what it means to be me, then and only then can I approach life on my terms. What do I mean by that?

Well, it is easy to react to a situation. It is easy to be rash. It takes more effort and being *intentional* to "center myself." When I am intentional in my actions and responses, I stop the drama that can come out of a bad situation. I get off the rollercoaster, if you will; I stop the ups and downs due to my inability to center myself, to be calm, to look at a situation for what it truly is rather than what I perceive it to be.

I am not talking about overthinking or not getting inside your own head. (I have been the queen of that.) No, I am talking about going to the very core of what makes me, well, me. Quiet my thoughts. Shut out the voices of self-doubt, fear, and disappointment. If I slow down, take in the full view and know within myself what I want, what I need, and act accordingly, I will find peace. I won't live in regret. I won't hurt myself or others by actions I never really took into account.

When I react, I have actually lost control. Rather than directing my own steps, I am basing my decisions off a situation or another person. I am no longer the influencer of my own life. I have given the power to something or someone else. They determine my happiness, my outcome, my view. I have it within myself to make my life what I want. I have been given the tools within myself to be all I was created to be. My passion, my desires, and my dreams are reliant only on me. No one can take from me that which I am. I have to willingly surrender it. And I am guilty of just that: giving up what I know to be true, or right, or what I want, and becoming a victim rather than a victor. It is a choice.

"Home is whenever I'm with you." This is the chorus to a song I heard recently. It brought up so many emotions. I was transported to times of laughing in the rain, holding hands, and losing myself in the moment of pure bliss. There is a fire that burns in me, and I believe in all of us, to be just who we are with another person—completely and totally us. It's like home. It's where we are safe. Home is where we go to escape from the world and all of its hardships. Home is where we go to rest and regroup. Home is where we go to just veg out, curl up on our couches and let nothing and no one bother us. Home is where we gather together to feed not just our bodies but our souls, the very essence of who we are. So how amazing is it to feel *that* with another being? It doesn't even have to be a romantic relationship. It just has to be real.

I have found that being real is not normal for a lot of people. They are used to the image of life. And when reality shows up, they freak out. They become fearful. They question whether what they are doing is right or not. I told someone I love the other day that reality is messy sometimes, and the messiness, the imperfection, is what makes it beautiful. It is a simple, deep calm, knowing inside of you that no matter what, you are safe to just be you. And that is what we all want: to be who we really are, not the image others may see or may want us to be.

1. *Unplugging from the hectic everyday of checking cell phones, seeing what others are doing on social media, and watching the unsettling news of the world we now live in and just playing in the rain, jumping the waves in the ocean, getting the sand in our hair and ears (a unique feeling for sure), and just absorbing true life.*

2. *Embracing the ones we love each and every day, regardless of what comes our way—yes, that is the feeling that electrifies me, that burns inside. "Home truly is whenever I am with you." May we all find home in ourselves if we do not have another to share it with yet.*

10
The Future

I have shared a lot about my journey to resetting my belief in myself. I wish I could have shared that it was easy and that it only took one bad relationship for me to change. What I discovered in my journey is that when you have a negative self-image, it extends past romantic lines. It is evident in work relationships and how you allow yourself to be treated by your boss, in family relationships when you don't draw boundaries, and in friendships where you give more than receive. Because self-hate is not just compartmental—it is across the board how you see yourself and how you feel about your worth. I believe I am more than I once thought. No, I know that I am more.

    I am hopeful that the future holds for me true love. I know one day I will experience sharing every day with my best friend and partner in life. Until that day comes, I am content to keep pursuing my dreams, solidifying my goals, and reaching for them. I will not waste time beating myself up for what I do not yet have; rather I will be grateful for what I am able to do now.

    I know that I truly have love for myself as never before, and

I can see the people in my life who love me. I can truly see who they are: my children, my friends, my family, and even some of the people I have had the honor of working with. Love comes from many different sources and it does not have to be romantic love in order to be felt and appreciated. I will not take for granted those who love me. I will not negate them because theirs isn't an amorous type of love.

I know there are those out there who will criticize what I have shared. They will not understand or comprehend what I am saying. They will judge and be harsh. But I am not at all worried about it. They are just blessed in that they have never felt the sting of rejection or the pain of verbal abuse. And let me be clear: when someone belittles you or causes you to feel less than, it is abuse. It is meant to harm, and it is not okay. We like to say it's not abuse. We like to say it's just being critical or harsh, because then we can excuse it and look the other way. But the very definition of abuse is to treat a person or an animal with cruelty or violence, especially regularly or repeatedly. Read that again: *regularly or repeatedly.* Abuse is meant to beat you down, to cause you to question your worth. And words are far more difficult to overcome than actual physical abuse. (I know as I have been at the hands of both types.) Words stay with you. They grow and evolve into this monster that controls how you see yourself. Words affect every part of you. That is why it is so important to know who you are. It is so important to protect yourself from it.

When my first book came out, I was a nervous wreck. I worried what people would think and say. I knew I had opened my heart up and exposed very intimate parts of myself. I had made myself vulnerable. And while there were haters, there were many more whose hearts were touched. There were many who reached out and asked for more.

The response I got was overwhelming. I actually cried when I realized that what I had gone through was helping others. There are more people who need what I have to say and share than there are who will judge.

It is not for me to be silent, to pretend I am okay, when I am not. It is not for me to endure pain at the hands of another because of that person's hurt. It is not for me to accept abuse and excuse it as my failure to love properly.

And it is not for you either.

If you find yourself currently in a relationship—work, intimate, or family—where you are not being respected, loved, or treated rightly, please find within yourself the strength to say no more. Know you are worthy of love. You are worthy of peace. You do *not* have to live a lie. You do *not* have to accommodate someone else's failures or take responsibility for him or her. You can find peace. Because you stay in an unhealthy relationship does not make you a martyr for love. It means you lack self-love. Set yourself free. Surround yourself with those who support you, who love you, and who will be there when it gets hard. And it will get hard. Leaving is just the first step. To actually make the move to never go back takes much more work. But you can do it!

I am blessed because I have a support system, one that never truly gave up on me, that challenged me to walk away, that made me choose myself, that encouraged me daily to keep choosing myself. It is a process. It is not a one-and-done kind of thing. You have to be intentional and determined. You have to have support.

I will do that for you if necessary. We never have to walk this alone.

Body image is about how we see ourselves. It extends to what we believe others see or don't see in us. Body image can be false. We can believe a lie if we choose to. We have to let go of the fantasy of what we think we should look like and begin to dance with who we truly are. We are each a masterpiece. We are each uniquely different from each other. That alone makes us special.

We can be shamed or praised for our bodies, but either way

is not an indicator of our worth. We are worthy simply because we exist. It took me many times to finally get this in my heart and accept it. There were many times when I chose what someone else thought or said over what I wanted. There were many times that I had given up on myself for another person. I agreed with the person's cruel words. I endured far more than I should have. I needed to love myself and I did not.

When we know who we are, when we accept who we are—good and bad—we will not be likely to allow another to cross the boundaries of defining us. We will have already done that.

It takes work. It takes dedication to you. But ultimately, you only truly have yourself. So be your own biggest cheerleader.

1. *What do you love about yourself? What is uniquely you? Write it down. Remind yourself daily of how special you are.*
2. *What are your goals? Write them down. Yes, I say write everything down. Why? Because it helps you to remember. You have to keep the vision in front of you or you will forget. You will get distracted. It's so easy to do.*
3. *What gifts do you have that you can work on perfecting in order to achieve those goals? What do you need to let go of to achieve those goals? Take the time you deserve for you. Give yourself grace. Extend love to yourself the way you have to others. Then sit back and enjoy just being the beautiful, wonderful person you are.*

Afterword

So much has happened. The highs have been incredibly high. The lows have been the lowest I've ever known.

There was not much middle ground. Nor much simple existence.

I was searching for the mundane. Hoping for the ease of everyday. A simplicity of being just loved. It was not to be found.

You see the relationship was just like an addiction. A drug.

I would feel the ecstasy of being alive. Being loved. Being showered with attention. Being intoxicated with the passion.

Only to come to the crashing of anger and arguments and feeling unworthy.

I put on the highest pedestal with praise and adulation, and then had the rug ripped out from under me being told how inadequate I truly was.

I was body shamed. I was ridiculed. I was accused of being unfaithful.

I was lied to and lied about.

I was left feeling confused and broken and unworthy.

The high was so much like I had never known that I would go back for more. Just to feel it again.

I knew that the end result would be painful. I knew that the high could only last so long, yet I was willing to experience the pain just for that brief moment of bliss.

It was what I lived for. It went from an addiction to an obsession.

I found myself isolating from those who loved me. I shut out their words of caution. I ignored their concern. I only focused on the feelings.

I was so afraid if I let go, I would never feel again. I would be stuck in the lowest place of being unworthy of love.

This wasn't love. This was merely lust—lust for something I should never have. A desire that could never be filled. A yearning and burning inside.

I found myself compromising. Letting go of all that I held important. I lost my standards for living. Gave up my expectations of what love really was—

All for the high. For brief moments in time.

This was the exact opposite of what my heart held hopes for—all I dreamed of—a constant, steady, true love. A quiet love. A peaceful life.

Love is about a knowing inside. It is safe. It is secure. You can count on it.

This was nothing like that.

This was volatile. It was fast. It had a fury in it. It had excitement. It held a mystery I could never solve.

SO, what kept me there so long? And what made me finally let go?

I wanted to prove my worth. I wanted to win the game. I wanted the passion and the excitement. I wanted to actually feel again. I had been numb for so long.

I had to let go. I had to release my grip—or let it release me. I had to quit dancing with the devil of destruction—because that is what I was doing.

I was destroying myself. I was disassembling all I had tried to become in this life. I was giving up. I was literally allowing myself to die from the inside out.

Letting go hurt more than holding on at first. It was like touching a hot stove—even when you remove your hand, you feel the intense sting of what you have done.

The decisions you have made. You blow on it hoping to soothe the pain. In the end time is the only thing that will ease the trauma.

Time. Patience. Being mindful. Accepting your part. Forgiving yourself. Moving on. Knowing you have learned your lesson and you do not need to look back in fear but choosing to look forward in hope.

CPSIA information can be obtained
at www.ICGtesting.com
Printed in the USA
LVHW102116290422
717237LV00024B/436